Make Your Own
Make It Go!

Make a

Roller Coaster

by Meg Gaertner

NORWOOD HOUSE PRESS

Norwood House Press
P.O. Box 316598
Chicago, Illinois 60631

For information regarding Norwood House Press, please visit our website at:
www.norwoodhousepress.com or call 866-565-2900.

LIBRARY OF CONGRESS CATALOGING-IN-PUBLICATION DATA

Names: Gaertner, Meg, author.
Title: Make a roller coaster / by Meg Gaertner.
Description: Chicago, Illinois : Norwood House Press, [2018] | Series: Make your own: make it go! | Includes bibliographical references and index.
Identifiers: LCCN 2018005352 (print) | LCCN 2018003229 (ebook) | ISBN 9781684041992 (ebook) | ISBN 9781599539270 (hardcover : alk. paper)
Subjects: LCSH: Roller coasters--Juvenile literature. | Amusement rides--Juvenile literature. | Handicraft--Juvenile literature.
Classification: LCC GV1860.R64 (print) | LCC GV1860.R64 G34 2018 (ebook) | DDC 791.06/8--dc23
LC record available at https://lccn.loc.gov/2018005352

312N—072018
Manufactured in the United States of America in North Mankato, Minnesota.

Contents

CHAPTER 1

All about Roller Coasters

People have been riding roller coasters for hundreds of years. The earliest known coasters were ice hills used as slides. One of the most famous early roller coasters was built in 1884. It was made of wood. It moved slowly along low hills. Today, roller coasters can move fast along huge hills. They twist and turn and move up and around loops. Using common household items, you can make a model roller coaster that will help you understand how full-size roller coasters work.

All roller coasters work the same way. They rely on **energy**. Energy is what gives things the ability to do work. Roller coaster cars do not have engines. Instead, a chain hooks onto the bottom of the car and pulls it up a slope. When the car reaches the top of the hill, the chain is released. The car then coasts along the rest of the track. Its movement depends entirely on its **potential energy**.

Potential energy is energy that is stored within an object. An object has potential energy because of its position. Objects that can easily move have lots of potential energy. This often has to do with **gravity**. Gravity is a force that pulls everything toward the center

A roller coaster must start by climbing a hill, otherwise it wouldn't travel very far.

of Earth. An object that is high up has a lot of potential energy. It has a great distance to fall before it hits the ground. This energy can turn into **kinetic energy**. Kinetic energy is the energy of moving objects.

Have you ever biked up a hill? You gain potential energy as you go up the hill. Once you go over the hill, the potential energy turns into

Some roller coasters turn riders upside down.

kinetic energy. Gravity pulls you down the hill. You can coast down without pedaling. The potential energy from the top of the hill turns into the kinetic energy of motion.

A roller coaster always starts with a large hill. The higher the hill, the more potential energy is stored in the car. The car **accelerates** down the hill. It moves faster and faster as gravity pulls it down. At the lowest point of the track, the car has no potential energy. But it has lots of kinetic energy. This energy gives the car the speed it needs to go up the second hill. As it goes up, the kinetic energy changes back to potential energy. The car slows down. It goes over the hill. It does this again and again. Your roller coaster will work the same way.

Some roller coasters have loops. The cars stay on the loop because of **centripetal force**. This keeps the car moving on a track that curves upside down. But cars must have enough speed to make it through a loop. A slow car would fall off the track when it reached the top of the loop. Modern roller coasters have safety rails to keep cars in place on the track.

Riders on a roller coaster feel the impact of gravity. It feels like a change in weight. When the car moves up a hill, it moves away from the pull of gravity. Riders feel heavy, like they are being pulled downward. When the car accelerates down a hill, it moves toward the pull of gravity. Riders feel weightless, like they could fly right out of their seats. These twists and turns make roller coasters fun and exciting. You can explore making hills, loops, twists, and turns in the model roller coaster that you will make.

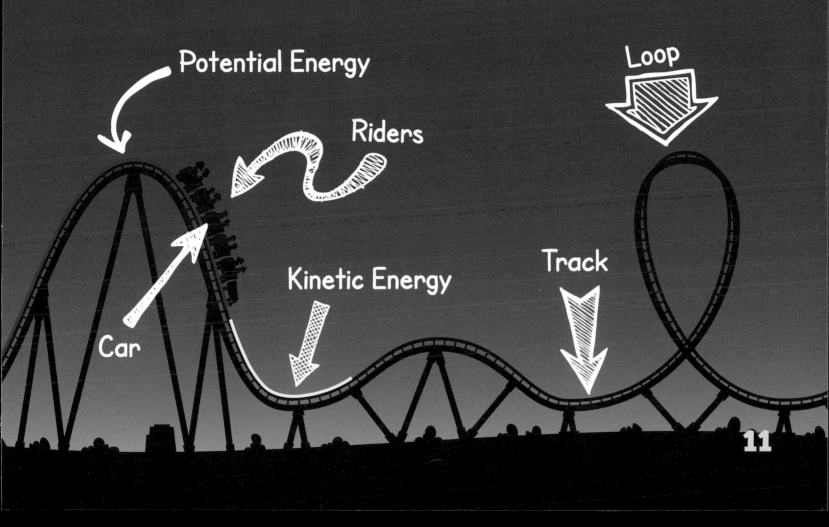

CHAPTER 2

Some roller coasters have riders in individual seats instead of cars.

Making a Roller Coaster

When making a roller coaster, engineers try to reduce **friction**. Friction is a force that takes energy away from an object's movement. When a roller coaster has friction, it slows down. There is more friction between rough surfaces than between smooth surfaces. This will be important to think about when you make your roller coaster.

For example, the car in your roller coaster should be small enough to fit in the track. It should also be smooth. A marble is small and smooth and will roll easily. It will make a good car for your roller coaster.

The track must be a smooth surface that curves easily. It must be wide enough so the car will fit. The track must also be sturdy so it does not fall apart when the car moves through it. Paper towel and toilet paper rolls are wide enough that a marble can move through them. But they do not bend easily. Also, many of them would have to be connected together to make a roller coaster. Each of those points of connection would slow the marble down. It would be better to have

Roller coasters are carefully made to make sure they are safe.

one smooth track. Foam insulation is long, hollow, and bendy. This would be a good choice for your track.

Your roller coaster must also be able to stand up. Beams can be made to hold the roller coaster in place. These beams will need to be made out of a strong material, such as cardboard. They will have to be taped to either side of the roller coaster. This is to make sure it does not fall over or lean to one side. The roller coaster can also be built against something solid, such as a wall. If the roller coaster is taped to a wall, the wall can hold it in place.

Once you choose the materials, you can map out your roller coaster. It must start with a tall hill. This will be the tallest hill of the

Riding a roller coaster can be a thrill!

entire ride. This will give the car all of the energy it needs to move along the track. After the first hill, the track can twist and turn, go upside down, or use smaller hills. Your roller coaster will start on a hill. It will also have a loop. Once you try this model, you can try adding other turns, hills, and loops in your next roller coaster.

To make a roller coaster, first prepare the materials for the track. Then, create the track with a starting hill and a loop. Next, make sure the track is sturdy and can stand on its own. Finally, place the marble at the beginning of the track and let it go!

Materials Checklist

- ✓ **6 feet (1.8 m) of foam pipe insulation**
- ✓ **Marbles**
- ✓ **Plastic cup**
- ✓ **Masking tape**
- ✓ **Measuring tape**
- ✓ **Scissors**

Because the foam is a smooth surface, the marble will fly down the track!

CHAPTER 3

Make It Go!

Now that you know how roller coasters work, let's put that knowledge to use and build one!

1. Cut the foam in half from one opening to the other opening. This gives you two long pieces of foam that can curve easily.

2. Find a bare wall. The wall will support your roller coaster.

3. Take one of your pieces of foam. Tape the top of your roller coaster onto the wall, 3 feet (1 m) from the ground. Tape it so that the foam curves up. This creates a track that your marble can fit in.

4. Create a loop with the other end of the foam. Tape this loop to the wall so it is 2 feet (0.6 m) high at its highest point. The roller coaster will run along the wall rather than move outward from the wall.

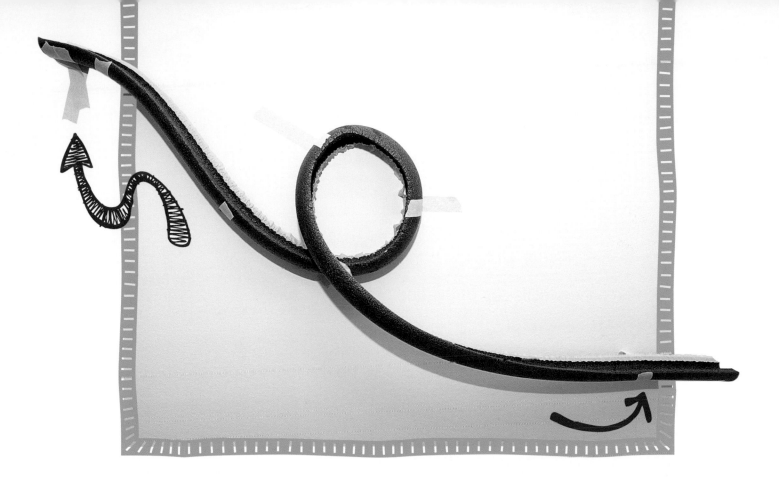

5. Tape the foam to the wall at other points throughout the roller coaster. This will make sure the roller coaster does not fall down.

6. Place the plastic cup at the end of the coaster. The marble will drop in here after it has finished the ride.

7. Hold your marble at the beginning of the roller coaster.

8. Let it go. Watch as the marble coasts through the ride!

28

Make It Better!

Congratulations! You built a roller coaster. Now see if there are ways to improve it. Use any of these changes and see how they improve your roller coaster.

- The first hill was 3 feet (1 m) from the ground. How would increasing the height of the first hill change the roller coaster?

- You used foam to build your roller coaster. What other materials could you use? How would those materials change the friction acting on the roller coaster?

Can you think of any ways that you could improve or change your roller coaster to work better?

Glossary

accelerates (ak-SEL-uh-rates): Moves faster and faster.

centripetal force (sen-TRIP-uh-tuhl FORSS): The force that acts on objects moving along a curve.

energy (EN-ur-jee): The ability to do work.

friction (FRIK-shuhn): A force that slows down objects that rub against each other, turning the objects' kinetic energy into heat.

gravity (GRAV-uh-tee): The force that pulls everything toward the center of the earth.

kinetic energy (ki-NET-ik EN-ur-jee): The energy of moving objects.

potential energy (puh-TEN-shuhl EN-ur-jee): The energy objects have due to their position.

For More Information

Books

Chris Oxlade, *Scientriffic: Roller Coaster Science.* San Diego, CA: Silver Dolphin Books, 2014. This book explains what roller coasters have to do with science and includes a fun activity for kids.

Tara Haelle, *Energy Exchange.* Vero Beach, FL: Rourke, 2017. This book describes where energy comes from and how it moves from one form to another.

Torrey Maloof, *Transferring Energy.* Huntington Beach, CA: Teacher Created Materials, 2016. This book describes how energy works and is transferred and includes a STEM activity for hands-on learning.

Websites

Amusement Park Physics: Design a Roller Coaster (learner.org/exhibits/parkphysics/coaster) Students can design their own roller coaster and learn how their choices affect how safe and fun the coaster is.

National Geographic Kids: Roller Coaster Videos (kids.nationalgeographic.com/explore/ youtube-playlist-pages/youtube-playlist-roller-coasters) This website includes carefully selected videos about roller coasters.

PBS Kids: Roller Coasters (pbskids.org/designsquad/video/roller-coasters) A mechanical engineer explains how to build a roller coaster in this video.

Index

About the Author

Meg Gaertner is a children's book author and editor who lives in Minnesota. When not writing, she enjoys dancing and spending time outdoors.